A

SERMON FOR THE TIMES;

PREACHED TO THE

First Church and Society in Stamford, Conn.,

APRIL 24th, 1853.

BY ISAAC JENNINGS.

PUBLISHED BY REQUEST.

NEW YORK:
S. W. BENEDICT, PRINTER, 16 SPRUCE STREET.
1853.

A

SERMON FOR THE TIMES;

PREACHED TO THE

First Church and Society in Stamford, Conn.,

APRIL 24th, 1853.

BY ISAAC JENNINGS.

PUBLISHED BY REQUEST.

NEW YORK:
S. W. BENEDICT, PRINTER, 16 SPRUCE STREET.
1853.

SERMON.

TRAIN UP A CHILD IN THE WAY HE SHOULD GO: AND WHEN HE IS OLD HE WILL NOT DEPART FROM IT.—*Prov.* 22 : 6.

"WHAT shall be done with the Slaves? and, what shall be done with the Young?" "These," said an eminent servant of God, in my hearing recently, "are the two great problems of this day." Weighty sentences, and worth repeating abroad. But, in order to a due solution of the former problem, must we not, first, attain to a due solution of the latter? "Suffer the little children to come unto me, and forbid them not; for of such is the kingdom of God." To draw from this oft-quoted, yet ever-beautiful saying of our Lord, that heaven is chiefly filled with those who *die* in early childhood, is not the most masterly interpretation of it. Rather, with those who *come to Jesus* in early childhood. But little children do not *come to Jesus* except they are *brought*. Indeed there would be no need of their coming to Jesus at all, if they could *begin* aright of themselves. The germs of sin, comparatively tender in infancy, grow if not duly attacked. They grow in youth; they grow in manhood.

When the body falters under the infirmities of old age, sin still lords it over the wasting powers, as desolation sits monarch upon old ruins. The vice of lying, for example. They are *privileged* parents, in whose children are never discovered the germs of this vice. So soon as it is seen, deal with it forthwith—resolve upon its destruction. The gardener, finding a worm at the root of a choice young tree, is not content to deal a few blows at the place, and thus leave it. His business is *to kill the worm*—to extirpate the evil. If the choice young tree has become crooked, he is not content to give it a few pulls in the right direction ; he carefully and perseveringly *trains* it into an erect posture. As the earth-wild is under the curse, so is human-*kind;* and if redeemed, to be so *with the Divine blessing*, by a faithful following of the rules laid down in God's word. There is then a radical difference between manufacturing a locomotive and training a *mind*—a *soul.* There is to be in the latter work, *Divine help*, in a sense in which such help is not necessary for manufacturing purposes.

I do not propose to furnish you with a system of rules, by which you can train your children, as the tailor has a set of rules by which to cut clothes for them. It is only by an exhibition of some very general considerations that I can hope to assist you in this work.

A supreme place must be given to the religious education of the child. Dr. South pithily remarks, that the people are " not to be *harangued* but *catechised* into principles." The Bible is allowed *as a reading book* in most common schools. But if *arithmetics were used only as reading books*, how much would the people know of the science of numbers, and of the art of computing by them ? It is true, to insist upon the teaching of religion in our common schools, might result in the teaching, to some extent, of a false religion, possibly in the destruction of our common school system. But what a confession ! The common school, so far as patronized, is virtually the principal place for the business of educating in childhood and early youth. Let its history lessons and its instruction in natural and moral science be given by persons who shall make these studies *to subserve the religious training* of the child, or else let the common school descend to a humbler sphere, in the great business of educating the young! Confine it to the department of teaching children to write, and cipher, and spell, and give it one day, or at the most two days, in the week for the purpose. *Or else—it were not desirable that common schools should be very common.* The Church of Rome is nearer right in *one* of her *premises* on this subject than are *some* American Protestants. She assumes that *all* the mental education of the child should be made subsidiary to its religious education. In this she is right. She would prevent the free study of the word of God. In this she is wrong. In this too—blessed be God—the solid Christian sentiment and feeling of this land is opposed to her. But in order to maintain this latter position against the Romish Church—what other policy so suicidal as to abandon the first, *i.e.*, the duty of making all studies subservient to religious education?

If it is true of the common schools, as at present constituted, that the Bible, if allowed at all, *is allowed only* as a reading book, then the same will be true *of the households generally, that send to such schools.* In the household, religion will be confined chiefly to the use of the Bible as a reading book, *and to a very meagre use. And the public exercises of religion must be made to conform.* The sermon, instead of being a faithful exposition, defence, and application of God's word, must be a handsome attempt to say something interesting, and at the same time *not to weary the mind or offend the feelings with any positive religious ideas. The people are not to be harangued*, but *catechised*, into *principles.* And *the* time for this catechising process is in childhood. "And thou shalt teach them," *i.e.*, the commandments of God in His Word, "diligently unto thy children; and shalt talk of them when thou sittest in thy house, and when thou walkest by the way, and when thou liest down, and when thou risest up." It is remarkable, that in some Bibles the marginal reading for our text gives "*catechise*," instead of "train;" catechise a "child up in the way he should go, and when he is old he will not depart from it." In order that arithmetic may be studied to good purpose, how much arduous labor of the mind is necessary? and to the whole circle of secular studies, how much *time* do our popular systems of education propose to devote? At least six good solid hours a day, for five days in the week—with the help of skilled and hired teachers. For the study of the word of God, on the contrary, *one hour, once in a week*. This, *to some extent*, is a true statement of the case of *Christian* households—and multitudes of children have not the one hour a week for their religious education. How long will it take by such a process to reach a state of the public mind when the Bible shall not be allowed as a reading book in our common schools? Even now, in Rhode Island, which for two years past has been held up as a model state on this subject, the commissioners of public schools have, it appears, decided that *prayer* cannot be made a part of the regular school exercises, *if any persons sending their children to the school object!*

In a very much admired address recently delivered in New York city, as reported, the speaker says: "The pious man's argument, that all should be taught to read, that they may read the Bible and inherit eternal life, is the very best of arguments for us as Christians; but for us as statesmen, it has no force whatever." Indeed! this is quite a phase of the modern refinements on this subject. How children shall be trained, so as to inherit eternal life, is a question "of no interest whatsoever" to us as statesmen. What are we living here on earth for? How are we prepared for the duties of time, except as we are mainly concerned to prepare for the retributions of eternity? And have we no interest, *as statesmen*, in seeing to it, that the children of this land are trained to please Him who is King of *kings*, as well as King in Zion? If so, let us first prove that a certain trite, but terse text, has no proper place in the word of God, viz. "Righteousness exalteth a nation, but sin is a reproach to any people." If we desire a well-built state, "we must build religion into the foundations of it," by training the children to be religious. I mean, of course, to be religious according to the word of God. If this cannot be done—if this is not done, either because we cannot agree what true religion is, or because we hate all religion, then may your hopes as a statesman, and your hopes as a Christian, for the ultimate prosperity of this nation, be given to the winds. *Mere* knowledge cannot save a people,—it must be knowledge of the *truth*. "The fear of the Lord, this is wisdom, and to depart from evil, this is understanding." It was not learning alone that gave being and power to the Reformation, but learned men, armed with the *doctrines of God's word*. It was the ninety-nine theses of Martin Luther. In other words, the positive statement of distinctive doctrines, in short sentences, which is so much scouted in these days. It was the vigorous enforcement in controversy of the great "abstractions," as some are pleased to call them, which lie at the basis of revealed truth. The cause of true religious freedom against the mighty power of Rome, is to be *saved* by the same means by which Luther and Calvin won it. It is true, the short method in a practical age, of overthrowing a corrupt religion, is to *show* its corruptions. But how shall the excellences of true religion be made to win votaries for herself, if the youth and the people are not thoroughly indoctrinated into her truths? Moreover, *Infidelity* is worse than Popery itself. The Church of Rome maintains public order, and that is more than Infidelity can do. The Church of Rome gave forth—unwillingly, indeed—a *Wickliffe* and a *Martin Luther*, and that is more than Infidelity can do. But *before* Infidelity reigns in this land, there is reason to fear the Church of Rome will. Most assuredly she will, if we have nothing better to array against her than common schools where religion is excluded. Our hope is in Christian denominations (*who agree that the word of God shall not be bound,*) giving themselves to the catechising of children, and to the inculcating, in other ways, of Bible truths. And if we cannot agree among ourselves what these truths fundamentally are, it were better to have controversy until we can. Controversy is better than a sacrifice of religion, under the stigma of "sectarianism," for the sake of peace. Strange that any should think to save the freedom of the word of God, by ignoring, for the sake of peace, the duty of inculcating, in *all schools* and elsewhere, positive religious doctrine. This is the most fatal, as it is the most insidious device of the adversary, to bind the word of God by the process which is professedly adopted to guard its freedom.

Children should be trained *to due reverence and submission.* The temper of the times is for superiors in age and station *to show especial deference to children.* "Thou shalt rise up before the hoary head and honor the face of the old man." In how few instances do we behold children manifesting an inbred reverence for age! Success in life is made to depend much upon popularity; and popularity depends much upon art and tact; and one master resource of this art and tact, is to flatter parents by taking undue notice of their children. As wealth increases, the temptation to indulge children increases also, as does every temptation to effeminacy. The wishes of children are consulted and their caprice. When the school teacher is severe and the child complains, the complaint, perhaps, is listened to, and as a consequence the child is withdrawn and placed elsewhere. If the child or the youth does not fancy the preacher, the over fond parent concludes that the preacher is not suited to the place he holds. It comes to pass that the children rule first their mothers and fathers, then the teacher and minister, and also, to a considerable extent, public affairs generally. That which was enumerated among certain grave calamities coming upon Judah, is being partially reproduced amongst us—"I will give children to be their princes, and babes shall rule over them." To open the house of God to any cause, occasion or speaker, under a specious plea of philanthropy, tends to destroy *due* reverence for the house of God. Much more, when for the sake of popular effect, institutions, precedents, and dignities are flippantly assailed. What is to be gained for any sound reform, if the basis of all order—a due reverence for law and government—is broken down in the public mind? By some speakers and lecturers it is assumed that the people of this land are better than their laws. Never was there a more erroneous or a more hurtful assumption. The people are not better than the laws—THE LAWS ARE BETTER THAN THE PEOPLE. *There is no need of extreme and revolutionary assaults upon our institutions* in order to secure desirable progress. We are not in Italy, nor are we under the vexatious despotism of a Charles the First. Reverence for institutions is not a master passion of this age and country. The broad bases and lofty monuments of our fathers' patriotism are not so *numerous* or *extensive*, that they must be *pulled down* to make *room* for necessary works of modern construction. Under the cruel despotism of Nero, Christians were commanded to reverence the laws of the emperor as to them the laws of God. "For they are God's ministers"—"the powers that be"—"attending continually upon this very thing." "Render to all their due; tribute to whom tribute is due, custom to whom custom, fear to whom fear, honor to whom honor." If communities could rely upon every station and superior relation in life, being so filled as that the *personal talents*, *influence* and *wisdom* of the person therein could secure all needed harmony and life—the case were different. Take an example for illustration—*the ministers of the Gospel.* If there be in the congregation due reverence for the word of God and for the house of God, and for the Lord's day, and for the office of the ministry as of divine appointment, a man without brilliant genius, if he be honest and faithful, will so expound the word of God, and uphold the stated ordinances of public worship, as to be strong in the internal virtue of his office and work. But if it be otherwise—if the respect of which I speak be wanting, the whole reliance of such a congregation is upon the commanding personal talents, genius and *charm* of the preacher. God has not authorised such a dependence. He has not furnished the men necessary for such an emergency. Where one man could succeed with such a congregation, one hundred would fail. In the long run, true unity, thought and power for good to any point upon such a policy *is impossible.* The same reasoning will hold good as applied to the school teacher, and to officers in town and state.

It has been well said, that in these United States, "Freedom is our inheritance, but Intelligent Obedience our peculiar want." May God preserve us from the spirit of *slavish* submission. But men who are not taught *due* reverence and submission in childhood, are the very men to submit when they ought not to:—the very men to yield to temptation when they ought to resist, and to come into bondage to their fellows when they ought to be free:—the very men to be made into tools and vassals for the Pope. The only kind of submission which God can accept—as exercised towards Himself directly, or, under Him, towards others, is a *cordial* submission—intelligent and free. It is then a grand attainment, when a child is trained to a habit of *sincerely* and *gracefully* submitting, in all cases when submission is incumbent according to the dictates of a conscience unfettered by passion and enlightened by God's word. This will make law-abiding citizens, and citizens that are capable of improving the laws. This will make minorities patient and satisfied, and majorities tolerant and condescending. This will fit for the harmony of Heaven, where one Supreme Will reigns over all created wills, and guides all with freedom and beauty, as the sun reigns with centripetal power over its attendant lesser orbs.

Let *Parents* insist upon due submission in *due time.* To the infant child how nearly does the parent stand in the stead of God! Hence perhaps it is that we find the command, "Honor thy father and mother," placed among the *first* five commands of the decalogue—in *that* great table of the law which has especial reference to the claims of *God.* Hence perhaps in Paul's epistle to Timothy *reverence of parents* is termed "*piety.*" If a cordial submission then to parental authority can be secured in the child, that child's piety towards God—its everlasting salvation, I had almost said—is secured.

"Children *are early to be taught* the first great lesson of God's moral government—'Not my will but thine be done.' The parent that loveth his child with the love that God requires, does not wait until the child has become a rebel of long standing, and by fixed habits of treason against lawful authority become obdurate. He takes him while young and tender, before he has learned the tactics of war, or acquired by practice the arts of self-defence. In no pitched battle does he allow him to conquer, or to come off doubtful as to the result, both claiming the victory and both provoking each other to wrath and future contests." "The parent has the power, and his is the right, and his is the responsibility."

Children should be trained *to self-denial.* On worldly accounts this is necessary. Few children who are born rich die so. Children must be taught to earn their bread, else they will not know how to preserve riches, much less how to live respectably and usefully without them. Nor should children be allowed to despise useful *manual* labor. If Cincinnatus were living in this day, and as of old, accustomed to dig in his little garden with his coat off, beardless boys amongst us would regard him, on that account, as quite beneath their respect. This notwithstanding the beautiful lectures we have upon the dignity of labor, and the fine compliments that are paid to the working-classes. When the doctrines of Epicurus were announced to Fabricius, that old Roman patriot and sage replied, "I can wish nothing worse for the *enemies* of my country, than that such doctrines should prevail among them." Alas! Epicurianism itself proved Rome's worst enemy. Luxury *ruined* what Carthaginian valor was unable to subdue. The work of Missions, too, is not prosecuted as it should be, because our customs require the expenditure of so much money upon ourselves, and unfit us for the more arduous service, to which we must be subjected, if laboring for Christ in other lands and climes. There grows up in such an age as this, a dependence upon large incomes, or rather bondage to them. Men must have thousands a year in order to sustain a "high social position"—to use a phrase, whose recent appearance amongst us is itself a 'sign' of the times. Men come to feel, in a sense, *obliged* "to make gold their hope, and to say unto the fine gold, Thou art my confidence." Under the stimulus of such a necessity, it is impossible but that success in money-making should be the standard of respectability, and the key to power. Under such a stimulus, how can that injunction of Christ be obeyed, "Take no thought saying, What shall we eat, and what shall we drink, and wherewithal shall we be clothed"? Under such a stimulus how can men duly heed the warning of the wise man, "He that maketh haste to be rich shall not be innocent"? Hence it comes to pass that the standard of honesty among "driving business-men" is accommodated indeed. Hence those deep public corruptions, which patriotic men are seeking to expose and to punish, at the capital of this country, and in the city of New York. Hence is so comparatively unknown amongst us that severe idea of the Christian life, which Christ expressed when he said, "Whosoever denieth not himself, and taketh not up his cross and followeth after me, cannot be my disciple."

In the case of young men, who *have* no other *honest* income but a slender salary,—without moral courage to be singular,—

required by the fashion of the times, to board in style, and dress in style, and ride in style, and to attend expensive places of amusement: how prodigious the temptation to *steal* from employers, or to contract debts they are unable to pay! Train up children to be *independent* by training them to be content with the daily earnings of their own faculties, powers and skill. When the Samnites came to Curius, on his Sabine farm, with their bribe of gold, they received for a reply, "I count it *my* glory *not* to possess gold, but to have power over those who do." He was seated by the fireside, with a wooden platter before him, roasting turnips in the ashes. Train each child to some particular useful avocation. Nor is Lord Bacon's rule upon this point unworthy of consideration—"Let parents choose betimes the vocation and courses they mean their children should take, for then they are most flexible, and let them not too much apply themselves to the dispositions of their children, as thinking they will take but to that which they have most mind to.

It is true, that if the aptness, or affection of the children be extraordinary, then it is not good to cross it, but generally the precept is good, "Optimum elige, suave et facile, illud faciet consuetudo," (Choose the best employment, and *habit* shall in due time make it pleasant, and easy to be pursued.) Assume that *valuable* studies cannot be "made easy" except to diligent self-application, and to a resolute will. Assume that mind cannot be *fed* on novels, magazines and newspapers, but on treatises, on *history*,—on "books that are books." Trained to a relish for the popular literature of this day, mind loses its self-respect—departs from the true end of intellectual culture; in other words, is no longer *quick-sighted*, and *far-sighted in the discernment of the truth*—is no longer hardy to war a good warfare for the truth—weeps momentarily over wrongs that *others* are alleged to perpetrate—laughs at the follies of others, but at the same time has little inclination to contribute to the general progress, by any *solid* attainment in *self*-culture or self-control. Train children to the desire of possessing real worth, by training them to respect real worth in others, whether in a humble or handsome garb, whether born in a hovel or in a palace.

The child should grow up in the exercise of a submitted and intelligent *love*, supreme towards God, and impartial towards man. We hear much about love in this day; benevolence—philanthropy—influencing men by love to love. This is all just, and most timely, if the terms be understood in a sense true to the teachings of the word of God,—and if the end be sought for by means that will succeed. Christ had a mission of good to men. Each child should be made to feel that he is on a mission of good—that his life is to be a life of doing good; the love that grasps the true welfare of others, as a motive to live and to toil for. Think of an angel's holy love. Think of a love that makes the soul forgetful of itself, through sympathetic and interested contrivings, to do others good. Think of one who is made *earnest* by love—diligent, active, laborious. Some are made earnest by covetousness; some by lust; some by jealousy and hate; some by fear. Think of one made earnest by none of these, but by love; and therefore forgiving towards an enemy,—therefore joyful in adversity,—therefore laborious when labors are unrequited by reward and praise: because forgetful of self, mindful of others' happiness, or sorrowing (if sorrowing at all) over another's woe. Think of a love that casteth out fear; a love that will not despair, because conscious that love must still reign, must yet subjugate selfishness, and give to truth a throne yet upon the ruins of error throughout the world. Jesus Christ is our perfect model for this, and he alone. But after this divine model should the child be trained. Here is a growing disposition, into which, with the help of Divine grace, the child is to be moulded. For such a moulding process is middle age, or old age, as good a time as early childhood? You will notice the absence of striking vices is not up to the standard. It is not enough that the tree be fair to look upon. There must be a purpose that it shall bear good fruit. The object is to be the setting out of a young missionary,—perhaps not to go to the heathen,—perhaps not even to be a preacher, but still to go forth and onward, upon a mission of active, effective and self-denying good-will :—onward and out into this world, where there yet remains so much work for love to perform.

www.ingramcontent.com/pod-product-compliance
Lightning Source LLC
LaVergne TN
LVHW020638110826
845149LV00004B/1267
* 9 7 8 1 4 1 8 1 9 0 8 0 4 *